Classroom Assessment

Middle School

by
Jennifer DeGraaf Tendero

Published by Milestone
an imprint of
Frank Schaffer Publications®

Author: Jennifer DeGraaf Tendero
Editor: Cary Malaski
Cover Artist: Lori Kibbey
Interior Designer: Megan Grimm
Interior Artist: Kay McCabe

Frank Schaffer Publications®

Milestone is an imprint of Frank Schaffer Publications.

Send all inquiries to:
Frank Schaffer Publications
3195 Wilson Drive NW
Grand Rapids, Michigan 49534

Classroom Assessment—Middle School

ISBN: 0-7696-4076-1

2 3 4 5 6 7 8 9 10 PAT 10 09 08 07 06 05

Table of Contents

Introduction

It is common knowledge that students have different learning styles. Some are verbal learners, some visual, some kinesthetic, and so on. Most of us possess more than one learning style. The most effective teachers use a variety of teaching methods to reach the most students in the most effective way. So it is with assessment. Just as there is no magic method to teaching kids, there is not just one way to assess them. If there were, we'd all be using it. There probably is, however, a better way to evaluate a student project than through a multiple-choice test. There is probably a better way to evaluate reading comprehension than through a book report. For every skill in every content area, there is an appropriate tool of assessment to use.

Assessment can help you understand *how* your students learn, *what* they are learning, and *how well* they're learning it.

At the outset, it's imperative to distinguish between *evaluating* and *grading*, and to determine what *assessment* really is. Evaluation and grading are often used synonymously, when in fact they are very different tools of assessment. "*Grading* looks at a discrete moment in the term in order to assign a mark to it. *Evaluating*, with a more student-centered developmental perspective, looks at the relationship of students' performance to their earlier efforts and their future possibilities." Moreover, "grading serves adults in their needs to assign students to groups, classes, grade levels, and colleges . . . while evaluation primarily serves students as it focuses on the students' growth and learning" (Milner and Milner, pp. 370, 371). *Assessment* is an instrument used for both grading and evaluating student work.

Introduction

Milner and Milner cite five functions—articulated by Moffet and Wagner (1976)—of evaluation. Evaluation should indicate:

- to the individual student how effectively he is communicating,

- to the parent how much the student is learning in school,

- to the teacher the needs of the student, for diagnosing and advising,

- to the administrator how good a job the teacher is doing, and

- to all parties how effectively the curriculum and materials reach their goals (Milner and Milner, p. 427).

Additionally, teachers evaluate mainly for two purposes:

1. To diagnose where a student is in terms of learning. This is called formative, or diagnostic, evaluation.

2. To evaluate what a student has learned after a unit or task. This is called summative evaluation (Gere et al., p. 240).

It is important to understand these distinctions because in addition to knowing *what* assessment tool to use on a given assignment, you should also know *why* you are using that particular tool, and toward what goal.

Grading and evaluating student work cause much consternation to teachers. In my early years of teaching in the New York City Public Schools, I remember being unsure of what assessment rubric I was supposed to follow when grading student writing. There was tremendous tension between the desire to grade on the amount of effort a student put into a piece of writing, and how much he had improved since the beginning of the year—especially considering the obstacles many of my students faced living in one of the poorest neighborhoods in the country—and to grade on the quality of a piece alone.

When I did try to grade on the quality of the work alone, I realized that I had a conceptual idea of what I thought an excellent piece of writing should look like. I tried to articulate it and translate it into criteria, but it was still my idea. But then one day I read a student's writing and my heart sank. Erica was never able to meet my standard for writing. At the beginning of the year, she said she hated reading. By the end, she had read thirty books and asked me for a list of summer reading that she could take to the library with her. Now that was progress! That was learning!

Introduction

How do you evaluate that? How do you measure growth and quality? How do you draw lines of assessment that don't get blurred by race and class and personal biases? I wish I knew. What I do know is that I've taught with teachers who evaluated student work based solely on growth and progress. I thought they were doing their students a disservice, that they were subconsciously lowering the bar, which was not, in the end, helpful; I still do. I've taught with teachers who seemed to disregard effort and held the bar so high no one could reach it. I thought those teachers did their students a disservice; I still do.

What I also know is that assessment needs to be fluid and dynamic if it is going to best meet the needs of your students. In this book, we'll look at several types of assessment: portfolios, learning logs, peer/self assessment, student/teacher interviews, and reading journals. This book is meant to be an overview of these types of assessment. It is not a prescription for how to implement them; nor is it an exhaustive discussion of assessment. It is only an introduction to the rudimentary uses of these tools. There are many more tools, many more uses. Figure 1 on page 7 lists some of the possible ways to evaluate student work and learning. I invite you to adapt them to your classroom. Some, such as observation, will be fairly simple to implement. Others, such as portfolios, will require much more planning and thought.

Examine each tool—hold it in your hand, imagine how you might use it, do some research and ask experienced colleagues about their best assessment practices, then take a swing. A tool is made to be useful and used. So also with assessment.

There is not enough space on these pages to write about the philosophical and pedagogical significance of each type of assessment. Nor is there space to do an exhaustive comparison, or even to discuss more than a few of them in depth. What I can do in these pages is take some of these tools out of the box, show you how I usually hold them, and tell a few stories about how I am learning to use them. If you try out these tools to see how they function, you'll learn that *the way things work is that eventually something catches*.[1] Something catches for your students, and something catches for you. Things work then.

[1]Graham (1997), "The Way Things Work," from *The Dream of the Unified Field*.

Some Tools to Evaluate Learning

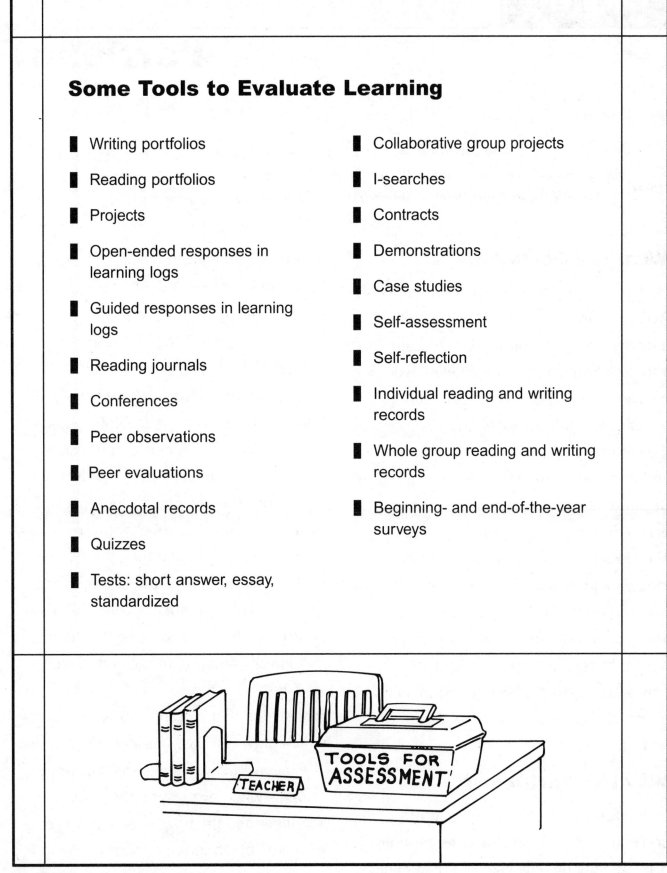

- Writing portfolios
- Reading portfolios
- Projects
- Open-ended responses in learning logs
- Guided responses in learning logs
- Reading journals
- Conferences
- Peer observations
- Peer evaluations
- Anecdotal records
- Quizzes
- Tests: short answer, essay, standardized

- Collaborative group projects
- I-searches
- Contracts
- Demonstrations
- Case studies
- Self-assessment
- Self-reflection
- Individual reading and writing records
- Whole group reading and writing records
- Beginning- and end-of-the-year surveys

Figure 1

Chapter 1

Portfolios

We cannot get a valid picture of a student's writing skill unless we look at more than one sample produced on more than one day in more than one mode or genre. . . .
– Peter Elbow, *Embracing Contraries: Explorations in Learning and Teaching*

What Is a Portfolio?

A portfolio is a collection of a student's work that documents his or her growth as a reader, writer, or thinker. It is not simply a folder of assignments completed over the course of a semester. Rather, a portfolio is a means for students to tell the stories of their learning, to reflect on their learning, and to demonstrate what they've learned. Because the story of learning is unique to each child, no two portfolios are alike. This does not mean, however, that there are no general guidelines for portfolios. Because portfolios have become the assessment tool du jour, they are in real danger of becoming standardized. When portfolio assessment becomes formulaic or mandatory, its essential usefulness will be lost.

Why Use Portfolios?

Portfolios remain one of the most powerful forms of assessment for writing because they directly engage the student in self-reflection and evaluation. They encourage students to become more thoughtful in their work and conscious of their learning. Portfolios also "make students more aware of their experiments and their specialties" (Graves, 1991).

The National Writing Project (NWP) has been at the forefront of developing and using portfolios. Teachers and researchers attend NWP Summer Institutes where they experience putting together portfolios of their own writing. This better prepares them to teach writing during the school year. Antonio Tendero, director of the *Lake Michigan Writing Project*, writes this about portfolios: "In my class, I see time flowing in a linear fashion until the end of the year. Portfolios reconstruct this linear progression to a looping recursive process which draws on past, present and future. The reconstruction moves the kids from students who have less control over deadlines and the flow of time to writers who are able to look both backward and forward in time at the writing that they have and will have in their portfolios."

Some Questions to Ask About Portfolios: Why and How Should We Use Them?

What kinds of portfolios?
English classes only?
Writing only?
Reading and writing?
All subjects?

What goes into a portfolio? Who decides this?

Who will grade the portfolios?
The classroom teacher?
A group of teachers in one department?
Teachers from all disciplines?
Students as well as teachers?
State or regional administrators?

How will portfolios be graded?
With one portfolio grade?
With one grade for the portfolio plus a grade for an individual piece
   of writing?
By evidence of student growth?
By individual pieces within the portfolio?

What are we assessing with these portfolios?
Evidence of student achievement?
Meeting standards set by school or state?
Student growth?
Ability of the student to reflect on his/her work?

How can we encourage self-reflection and self-evaluation in portfolios?
Introduction?
Have students reflect on each piece, or write one reflection for the portfolio?
Will the self-reflection and self-evaluation be written, oral, or both?

Figure 2
(Adapted from Claggett, 1996).

What Goes into a Portfolio?

If you've never used portfolios in your classroom, or if the use of portfolios is new to your school, I encourage you to get together with a group of teachers and carefully think through the questions posed in Figure 2 (page 9). These questions should help you determine *who* is going to use portfolios, *what* will go into them, and *how* they will be evaluated. But these questions assume that you have already answered the question, "Why am I using portfolios in my classroom?" If you have not already answered this question, do so before moving on to anything else. Parents, administrators, and students will inevitably ask you this question. More importantly, you should ask it yourself.

Once you have constructed a framework for portfolios in your curriculum, you'll need to know what goes into them. The following pieces are typically included in portfolios:

An introduction—Much like the introduction to a novel, the introduction to the portfolio gives a student space to reflect on her work.

It also serves to contextualize the body of work for the reader. Whether you call it an introduction or a cover letter, the goal is similar for both.

Writing the introduction involves the student in a key component of authentic portfolio assessment: self-reflection. If the process of assembling a portfolio is an act of self-reflection, then the introduction is a sort of meta-reflection on the entire collection, offering a rationale for the inclusion of certain pieces and reflecting on the process of putting together the portfolio. An introduction gives the student a chance to reflect on her learning.

An introduction does not have to be long. Depending on the number of pieces included in the portfolio, a well-crafted page or so is usually sufficient. Additionally, some teachers will ask students to write a cover sheet for each piece of writing included in the portfolio.

Several pieces of writing that represent the student's very best work—These pieces showcase the best a student has to offer. For each piece of writing, a student should reflect on what she has done well in that particular piece and why she chose it.

The pieces chosen should include different genres and writing styles. You will not be able to fairly evaluate a portfolio that only includes fantasy short stories. The idea of portfolio assessment is to gather together a diverse sampling of student work. This will be best accomplished by having the teacher mandate the inclusion of some pieces, and having the student determine the inclusion of others.

One best piece of writing that includes all drafts of that piece—This will reveal the student's process of writing. Students used to turn in final drafts, which were evaluated and graded as entities unto themselves, as if they had no predecessors, as if there were no process. Teachers graded with the dreaded red pen, often more interested in grammatical perfection than content. It didn't much matter what you wrote, as long as you wrote it correctly.

We know better now. We know that the process of writing and learning is nearly as important in evaluation as the final product. It is so important to look at a student's process of writing, and for both student and teacher to reflect on the learning that took place in that process from seed idea to published work. Therefore, include all drafts, revisions, editing, and evaluations of that piece.

It is helpful to have the student write a rationale for including this piece. The rationale explains why she selected that particular piece of work, what standards she used in selecting it, an honest evaluation of that piece, and a clear defense that shows why she believes this piece is her best.

> **Tip:** Because students don't know at the beginning of the year what pieces they will be including in their portfolio, have them save all drafts of every piece they write. Often, the seed of a great idea can be found in a discarded draft.

To help make the process of assembling portfolios easier, I have my students keep Individual Writing Records (Figure 3, page 14). These document what they have written, who helped them with editing and revising their writing, and what point in the writing process they've reached with each piece. Students keep these in their writing folders and we occasionally look at them together to see if we notice any patterns in their writing. For example, if an Individual Writing Record shows that a student wrote first drafts only of six pieces of writing and didn't take any of them through to the process of publication, this tells me that there is something about her writing style that we should address. If I notice that a student publishes every piece he's ever written, he might need to slow down and spend more time on revising.

In a series of mini-lessons, I talk about how to choose not only which pieces to take to the next step, but which pieces to abandon. When my students are deciding on a topic, I tell them to research and write about something so intriguing that it will keep them up at night. This advice usually steers them toward a topic that they can successfully take all the way through the writing process.

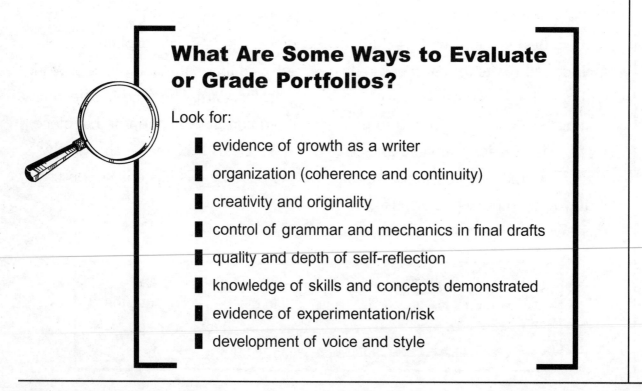

What Are Some Ways to Evaluate or Grade Portfolios?

Look for:

- evidence of growth as a writer
- organization (coherence and continuity)
- creativity and originality
- control of grammar and mechanics in final drafts
- quality and depth of self-reflection
- knowledge of skills and concepts demonstrated
- evidence of experimentation/risk
- development of voice and style

Some teachers give two grades for each portfolio: a *portfolio grade*, which evaluates how much work, risk-taking, and revising students have put into their portfolios; and a *single grade* that evaluates one piece of writing.

Some prefer giving one grade to the portfolio as a whole. Figure 4, titled Criteria for a Good Portfolio (page 15), shows several criteria used to come up with one portfolio grade.

Not every portfolio should be evaluated using all these criteria, and not all criteria need to be determined by teachers. When teachers and students collaborate in determining criteria for evaluation, the evaluation is more authentic because students feel ownership not only of the contents, but also of the evaluation process. Further, having teams of teachers evaluate portfolios together lends a richness to the evaluation that is absent when one teacher evaluates alone.

Having a portfolio conference with a student adds yet another layer of ownership to the process by offering further opportunity to take stock of the work he's done, and to better understand how he's developed as a writer.

Portfolios Across the Curriculum

Portfolios are not used exclusively for students' writing, nor are they used only in the English classroom. In Smith and Juska's *The Whole Story: Teachers Talk About Portfolios*, you can read compelling stories of how National Writing Project teachers use portfolios in their English, biology, and history classes; what it takes to set up a portfolio system; what a "portfolio classroom" might look like; and how teachers prepare students to create portfolios. Donald Graves (1991) has written extensively about reading portfolios in the early elementary grades in *The Reading/Writing Teacher's Companion: Build a Literate Classroom*. Both of these books are wonderful resources to use before incorporating portfolios into your classroom.

Individual Writing Record for _____

#	Title	Genre	Peer-conference with:	Date finished	Edited by:	Date published
1						
2						
3						
4						
5						
6						
7						
8						
9						
10						
11						
12						
13						
14						
15						
16						
17						
18						
19						
20						
21						
22						
23						
24						

Figure 3 (Adapted from Atwell, 1998).

Criteria for a Good Portfolio

Name _____

1. Growth/Progress
   ___ multiple drafts of each finished piece
   ___ evidence of thoughtful revision, not just editing
   ___ evidence of experimentation and risk-taking

2. Sense of Purpose
   ___ introduction/cover letter that clearly introduces the portfolio
   ___ evidence in the introduction/cover letter of growth as a writer

3. ___ Ability to finalize and publish different genres of writing

4. Shows Variety and Experimentation
   ___ writing has a developing style
   ___ each piece shows clear points of view
   ___ writer is developing a tone unique to him or her
   ___ writer is able to write in several different genres

5. Follows Instructions
   ___ portfolio is organized and follows guidelines
   ___ introduction/cover letter follows guidelines

6. Conventions
   ___ final drafts have been peer- and self-edited
   ___ final drafts show control of usage and conventions

7. Reflection
   ___ evidence of thoughtful reflection(s) about the writing process, process of choosing what to put into the portfolio, and process of assembling the portfolio

Figure 4

Chapter 2

Rubrics

If portfolios are graded as a whole, or perhaps given a portfolio grade and a grade on a single piece of writing, how do we assess individual pieces of writing? In as many ways as you can count, actually. Teachers today do not always have the liberty to create the rubric by which students' writing is evaluated. Each state has set standards and rubrics for writing, which teachers must follow for a number of reasons. Having said that, these rubrics mean virtually nothing without teachers to adapt and apply them to their classrooms. Unless teachers—and their students—act as interpreters of the language of state standards, the standards lose their intended purpose. This is both fortunate and unfortunate for teachers; it's fortunate because the standards afford quite a bit of latitude for personal interpretation and classroom application. It's unfortunate because teachers don't always understand exactly what it is their students are expected to know in order to meet state standards. This confusion, combined with the urgency for each school to make Adequate Yearly Progress or risk losing federal funding, has some teachers abandoning best practices in favor of teaching to the test. This is not necessary; teaching does not have to be dichotomized in this way.

The National Writing Project has been one of the comprehensive school reform programs recognized by the *No Child Left Behind* reform catalogue. Figure 5 (page 17) shows how the teachers at one school in Michigan learned to collaboratively assess student writing with the goal of making Adequate Yearly Progress in writing achievement. The protocol they followed was adapted from Steve Seidel's *Project Zero* in Cambridge, Massachusetts, in which thirty educators convene once a month for a "Collaborative Assessment Conference." At each conference, one educator presents student work he has brought, which is read and discussed by all. The goals of these conferences are to encourage conversations between teachers, to see student strengths as well as weaknesses, and to demonstrate all that can be seen in a single student's work (McDonald et al., 2003). While not directly comparing the student's work to standards, "it involves standards—implicitly but purposefully" (McDonald, p. 77). This assessment was made by groups of teachers, but can be adapted in your classroom with collaborative groups responding to and assessing each other's writing in turn.

Collaborative Assessment Protocol:
Looking at Student Work in Light of the Rubric

Steps

1. *Presenting.* Participant presents a single student's work, offering only minimal context. Participants read silently, marking on their copies any sections that hold particular significance for them.

2. *Describing.* "What do you see?" Group members respond by describing components or aspects of the work without making judgments of quality.

3. *Raising Questions.* "What questions does this work raise for you?" Participants respond with questions they have about the student, the work, the assignment, etc. During this time, the presenter listens and makes notes, but does not respond.

4. *Speculating.* "What do you think this writer is working on?" Responders say what they think the writer was attempting to learn, accomplish, practice, or improve.

5. *Responding.* The presenter speaks and has a chance to respond to questions raised, to offer additional context, and to share any surprising feedback heard during the earlier steps.

6. *Reflecting and Discussing.* "Keeping in mind our state's rubric, how does this inform your next steps of teaching?"
   (LMWP, 2004)

Figure 5

As the year progresses, the rubric naturally shifts to accommodate what students learn about effective writing. I think students better absorb information when it is layered in this way, when expectations for their quality of writing grow as they learn more. When it comes time to take the writing test, they are familiar with the rubric, comfortable with the writing process, and ready to show they know how to write well.

Figure 6 (below) shows a rubric for a first-semester piece of writing. This rubric addresses standards while also reflecting the specific elements of effective writing that a teacher might introduce as a base for this and all future pieces of writing.

Rubric for Writing Workshop Piece # 1

Writer's Name _____

These are the editing and revising techniques we've discussed in class. I expect you to use these in writing this piece and in future writing.

___ Writing has an effective lead that draws the reader into the piece and makes him want to keep reading.

___ Writing includes relevant information that does not overwhelm the reader and answers the 5 Ws and 1 H—who, what, when, where, why, and how.

___ Writing tells just one story, not several.

___ Writing shows evidence of thoughtful revision; every attempt has been made to improve your writing with each new draft. Revision reflects suggestions from peer conferences.

___ Writing is carefully edited by you as the author and by another editor, using standard editing techniques.

___ Final draft is typed, with few or no mistakes.

Figure 6

Figure 7 (page 20) features questions you might want to consider when creating a rubric with your students. Working in small groups, give each group a worksheet along with a sample of whatever it is you want them to create a rubric for. Come together as a whole class and create a rubric from the work they've done in their small groups.

Before evaluating student writing based on criteria, it's helpful to decide whether you will evaluate it holistically or analytically. **Holistic evaluation** judges a piece of writing as a whole and gives it a grade that represents an overall impression, usually in comparison with other papers in a group. **Analytical evaluation** may employ any given number of criteria, but these criteria will be spelled out (Gere et al., p. 260). The sample rubric on page 20 uses specific criteria and is designed to evaluate student writing analytically.

Deciding not only how you will evaluate student writing, but also by what method, is no small task for the middle school teacher. Your philosophy of teaching will be most transparent in how you choose to evaluate student work.

Questions to Consider When Creating a Rubric

1. What is your main objective? In other words, what are students expected to know and demonstrate they know? List no more than four main concepts.

   1. _____
   2. _____
   3. _____
   4. _____

2. How will you determine that students really know what they know? For each main concept above, name a specific criterion to be demonstrated by students.

   1. _____
   2. _____
   3. _____
   4. _____

3. Create a rubric for each criterion using clear and simple language.

   1. _____
   2. _____
   3. _____
   4. _____

Sample

Objective: Students can clearly retell the events of a story in a summary paragraph.

Criterion: Retelling is using one paragraph to incorporate main events and actions in that section of the story.

1	2	3
Retelling has little to do with events in the story.	Retells events in the story but is not concise; doesn't identify main events.	Concisely retells main events in the story.

Figure 7

Chapter 3

Observation

"Teachers are in a particularly privileged position to observe children in the process of learning. This is because children undertake so many of their learning activities in the presence of the teacher, and because teachers are uniquely trained to understand the behaviors that are observed" (Anthony et al., 1991).

Observation is what every teacher does, every day. From the moment our students enter the classroom, we observe their behavior, their collective mood, their energy level. Some days the collective mood of the students necessitates a shift in our lesson plans; we shorten one activity, lengthen another, omit one altogether. Sometimes our observations lead us to invite our students to open a favorite book and read silently, or to listen as we read to them. Other days, it seems as if everybody is half-asleep, and a few minutes of stretching and wiggling around invigorates our students. Some days we're too busy to observe, and we wish we had. Our students act, speak, gesture; we observe, shift, ask them to shift. This is part of the dance that every decent teacher engages in with his or her students.

That kind of observation is essential to the classroom. It's what makes the classroom work. There are other kinds of observation, though, that are equally important in assessing how children learn and in determining the extent to which children are engaged in their learning. The three main kinds of observational assessments are **whole group, small (or cooperative) group,** and **individual**.

Whole Group Observation

It's one thing to put a finger on the pulse of your students from minute to minute, day to day. It's quite another to use that observation in assessment. While whole group assessment is not usually used for grading purposes, it is important for a teacher to understand how to make educated observations of her or his class.

Observing your class is a skill that comes with practice. Good veteran teachers seem to do this automatically; and, to some extent, they do, simply because they've been at it so long. Newer teachers often miss the opportunity to assess their class by observing, usually because they're overwhelmed with the newness of teaching and all it requires. A veteran teacher can often observe a classroom for five minutes and tell you quite accurately whether or not the students are engaged in learning and whether they understand what they're being taught. The teacher then adjusts his expectations, or what he's doing, or how he's doing it based on what he's observed. How? Let's look at an example.

Mr. Murphy is reading to his students. He is sitting in the author's chair, and the students are sitting on carpet squares on the floor around him. It is Authors' Celebration Day, in which students share their published writing with each other. Mr. Murphy wants his students to have fun because they've worked hard to get to this day. But before he even came into the classroom, he knew he'd have to keep a tight structure with his kids so the celebration wouldn't get out of hand. During the course of the hour-long celebration, he is constantly observing his students, and makes a number of adjustments accordingly so that the Authors' Celebration Day runs smoothly.

Many times, teachers don't need to have their students in front of them in order to observe and assess. Ms. Ramos is grading the test on Medieval Europe she just gave her eighth graders. More than half of them have failed, and Ms. Ramos is understandably frustrated by this. If she is an observant teacher, she'll need to ask herself some hard questions in order to understand why so many failed. Is the timing of the test to blame? Was the format different from previous tests she's given and therefore not familiar to her students? Did she prepare her students well enough to be successful on the test? Did she rush through the material or assume her students had background knowledge they didn't possess? If she believes none of these caused her students to fail, it might be safe to assume that the students did not study enough.

Observational assessment is not an exact science; authentic assessment rarely is. But the observant teacher who is in tune with her students will be able to analyze the learning behaviors of her students and use her observations to tweak her teaching strategies to best fit their needs and meet the goals she's set for her class.

Cooperative Group Observation

Students learn best in a variety of situations within a classroom. Teachers who allow for individual, small group, and whole group learning opportunities offer their students the best of all worlds.

Small (or cooperative) groups work when the "teacher sets students on a more independent course so that group discoveries are made without the direct intervention of the teacher. Cooperative learning invites students to explore ideas, to wrestle with new information, and to make sense of the changing experience" (Milner and Milner, 1993).

The main role of a teacher in cooperative groups is to get students started, and then to observe what happens as the group interacts and learns together. It is naïve to assume that having settled the students in their groups, you as the teacher are free to work at your desk or catch up on grading. Kids sense when a teacher is disengaged from her class, quickly veer off task, and things fall apart with surprising ease. To prevent this, some teachers circulate slowly among the groups, making notes on a clipboard. The process of working together is valued and graded along with the final product, whatever that may be.

In effective cooperative groups, students have meaningful roles so that each lends something to the process of group learning and discovery. These roles should be rotated so everyone gets a chance to contribute in a different way.

Mr. Nguyen's students are discussing in cooperative groups the result of a lab they just completed in his sixth grade science class. Malik is the facilitator for the day. It is not his job to teach or to lead the discussion. It is his job to guide it by making sure everyone contributes and no one dominates the conversation. After they've been talking for a few minutes, Mr. Nguyen observes that Mary is not saying anything. He watches for a few more minutes, then walks over to the group and gently reminds Malik that part of his job is to ask everyone to contribute. If Mr. Nguyen were to sit at his desk and check his email after speaking to that cooperative group, chances are nothing would change. But Mary knows her teacher has been observing her role in the group, is referring to her, will continue to observe their group, and will speak directly to her if she doesn't start contributing. She rolls her eyes and reluctantly begins to participate. Mr. Nguyen makes a note on his clipboard to ask Mary to facilitate their next discussion in order to more fully draw her into the group.

The observations Mr. Nguyen is making are spontaneous. He does not have one particular objective in observing the small groups. Instead, he is observing his students to make sure they are engaged with each other and on task. At another point in the semester, he will sit down with his clipboard and a participation chart and assess his students for a set of specific behaviors. Students like Mary often get overlooked in a group of more verbal students. A participation chart can alert a teacher to developing antagonisms or dysfunction within a group.

Individual Observation

Circulating the room with a clipboard and a checklist is an excellent way for teachers to observe how individuals behave in collaborative groups. A checklist can include a rubric of expected behaviors, or it can be more anecdotal, simply recording behaviors you observe without inserting your opinions about them. "Melissa is being disruptive in her small group," is not an example of an anecdotal record because you're making a judgment about her behavior. "Melissa is playing with Yessenia's hair and giggling," is an example of an anecdotal record. You might want to have a sheet for each student on which to write your observations.

Research shows that observation is most effective when it's focused and single-minded. Before you observe individual students, decide what you're specifically looking for: a behavior, a skill, participation, or an attitude. This not only makes observation easier, but it also brings a fairness to the assessment. Putting behaviors and attitudes on a continuum, such as *speaks willingly . . . speaks reluctantly,*

simplifies this process even further. Figure 8 (page 26) shows a sample observation chart.

Peer- and Self-Observation

Some of the best and most honest observations often come from students themselves, especially when they've had a hand in creating the rubric. Students love taking anecdotal records; most of them naturally observe more than you think they do. Assign a student to observe the peers in her collaborative group for one class period. Collect her observation sheet and make copies for everyone in her group. During the next class, invite the group to study the observation sheet and learn about how they function as a group based on their peer's observations.

If one of your goals is to make students into lifelong learners, then teaching them to be reflective is a smart way to accomplish this. The reflection that's done in portfolios is a type of observation of the self as learner. As an assessment tool, observation can be used to both look out—when the teacher is observing her student—and look in—when the student is observing himself.

Observation Checklist

Date _____

Learning Situation _____

Behavior/Skill/Attitude I'm Observing _____

	Student	What I Observed	Action?
1.			
2.			
3.			
4.			
5.			
6.			
7.			
8.			
9.			
10.			

Figure 8

Chapter 4

Self-Evaluation

I always keep the reading and writing surveys my students complete at the beginning of the year. We pull them out in June after they've completed an end-of-the-year reading and writing survey (Figure 9, pages 29–30). Students study them to see how their views of themselves as readers and writers have shifted over the course of the year. I have taught them everything I can; I have worked hard to convey my love of reading and language by reading books aloud to them, by sharing a poem every day, by giving them space and time during class to read books they choose. In the end, though, they're the only ones who can determine how much they've changed. Some might even argue they're the only ones who know how much they've learned. This doesn't mean I haven't assessed their learning throughout the year, because I have.

But self-evaluation has a special role inside and outside the classroom. We often think of assessment as something that comes at the end of the learning process and has a grade attached to it. But students need to be encouraged to engage in constant self-evaluation as they're learning. The value of self-evaluation lies in the shift from external to internal; it "locates evaluation within the individual where it must reside for the life of the learner apart from school" (Milner and Milner, 1993). We say we teach writing, but our end goal is to teach students to evaluate themselves by constantly questioning their work, their comprehension, and the effectiveness of what they're trying to communicate. The best writers spend a lot of time reading over and thinking about what they've written so far and considering where they might go next.

"What is it I'm trying to say here?" "Do I have too much information? Too little?" "Is my writing honest?" (Atwell, 1998).

The best readers also engage in this self-evaluation before, during, and after reading. Whether your students are reading a novel, a poem, or a chapter on the American Revolution, they should be asking questions:

"What do I already know about this topic?" "Do I understand what I'm reading?" "What do I need to do in order to understand it?" "What parts seem important to remember?" "Why do I find this section disturbing?"

This type of self-evaluation is ongoing in the best students and absent in those who most struggle.

Implementing Self-Evaluation in Your Class

▮ Encourage your students to ask themselves questions while they're reading or writing.

▮ Conduct a series of mini-lessons on reading fluency, which is applicable across the curriculum. Ask students to assess and set reading fluency goals for themselves and revisit throughout the year (Figure 10, page 31).

▮ Model self-evaluation when you're reading to them by wondering and questioning aloud.

▮ Engage students in meta-evaluation by asking them to evaluate how well and how often they evaluate their learning. (The concept of metacognitive thinking is understandable when students realize it's simply thinking about their thinking.)

▮ Have your students create rubrics for projects, papers, and speeches.

▮ Have students complete a learning inventory at the beginning and end of the semester or year. The student gives his or her opinions, attitudes, prior knowledge, and interest in the subject at hand.

▮ Learning logs have a component of self-evaluation in them. We'll explore how to use learning logs in a subsequent chapter.

▮ Have students tell the story of their experience in your class: What was the most important thing they learned? The least important? How did they grow as a thinker? What topic would they have liked to explore further? Figure 11 (page 32) is an example of a letter inviting students to engage in self-evaluation.

▮ Each time they complete a draft of a piece of writing, have the students evaluate their writing by completing an evaluation sheet.

▮ Have students complete a midterm evaluation report that asks them to evaluate their work so far, and invites them to revisit their goals for the semester.

Your educational goals and grades you give will be clearer to your students if you involve them in the evaluation process. This is a departure from traditional education where the adult is the sole evaluator in the classroom. Self-evaluation answers two basic student questions: "How am I doing?" and "Where do I go from here?" Equally important, it empowers students, values the process of learning, and engages students in kinds of metacognitive work they'll need to do for the rest of their lives.

End-of-the-Year Self-Evaluation

Name _____ Date _____

1. How many books did you finish this semester? _____

2. What genres did you read? _____
    _____

3. How many literary letters did you write? _____

4. Of the books you read on your own, which was your favorite?
    _____

5. Of the books we read together as a class, which was your favorite?
    _____
    _____

6. Which book did you least enjoy? Why? _____
    _____

7. Who is your favorite author(s)? Why? _____
    _____

8. Who is your favorite poet(s)? Why? _____
    _____

9. What are you proud of accomplishing in your reading this year?
    _____
    _____

10. What reading habits, if any, from this year will you continue to do?
    _____
    _____

11. How many pieces of writing did you finish this year? _____

End-of-the-Year Self-Evaluation, cont.

Name _____ Date _____

12. What genres did you use in your writing? _____
_____

13. What piece was your best? Why? _____
_____

14. What piece of writing most challenged you? _____
_____

15. In what ways do you think you grew as a writer this year? _____
_____

16. What conventions did you learn to use in your writing? _____
_____

17. If you were the teacher, what four books would you read in class next year?
_____
_____

    Explain why you'd choose them. _____
_____

18. Did your attitude toward reading and writing change this year?
    Why or why not? _____
_____
_____

19. Grade yourself on the effort you put into this class. _____ Write a short
    defense for this grade. _____
_____

Figure 9

0-7696-4076-1 *Classroom Assessment*

Goals for Fluent Readers

Name _____ Date _____

1. Read more and read often.

2. Read for larger blocks of time before stopping. Try to pick up groups of words (chunks of meaning) rather than individual words.

3. Try to concentrate on key words that carry the meaning. Researchers call these *contentives*. Research shows that good readers fix longer on words that carry meaning in the sentence.

4. Work to eliminate bad habits:

    ▪ moving your lips

    ▪ regressing: constantly going back to reread something you've already read

    ▪ using a pencil or card to "underline" each line you read

All of these bad habits slow down your reading, forcing you to pick up single words instead of reading for meaning. Forge ahead. Speed increases comprehension because it diminishes distraction. Count on the context that's built into the text to help you understand what you're reading.

5. Time yourself as a reader. How many pages can you read in 30 minutes this month? By December? By the end of the school year?

Given what you now know, what are your personal goals as a reader?

1.

2.

3.

Figure 10 (Adapted from Atwell, 1998).

Dear Eighth Graders,

I've been thinking a lot about the ending of the year, which signals so many things: your graduation from middle school, a pause for me from teaching, and final examinations, among others. I have been wondering what your examination should look like.

I've come up with this: What I really want you to do is to reflect. Reflecting on where you've been and what you've learned is a part of discovering what you love and don't love, and who you are as a student. In terms of a response to literature, or an essay on the themes of all the novels we've studied, there is very little I could ask you to do that would teach you just one more thing in the hopes of making you just a little bit smarter. You have already proven what sort of students you are, and most of you have worked extremely hard this year— almost all of you met or exceeded the reading requirement. Bravo! Your writing is another area in which I have seen growth in many of you; I can't wait to finish reading and responding to your portfolios. I have tried to provide a rigorous course of study for you; I hope I have. Now it's time for you to look rigorously at the work you've done this year. How should this reflection look and what should it contain? Here are some ideas:

- Write about how you have changed as a reader. How have you grown as a reader, what have you tried that's new for you? What would you like to read over the summer?

- Reflect on how your writing has changed—what you've learned about yourself as a writer/poet, and what you still want to work on.

- How have you grown as a learner? In what ways do you feel ready—or not—for high school?

- What will you most take away from our study of literature of early Europe? What was your favorite thing we did? What did you like the least?

- What didn't you say or question in class that you wish you had?

Of course, reflecting on these means shaping them into cohesive paragraphs of thought that demonstrate introspection. Choose a few that resonate with you.

Yours,
Jennifer D. Tendero

Experience is not what happens to you; it is what
you do with what happens to you.
—Aldous Huxley

Figure 11

Chapter 5

Conferencing with Parents and Students

Conferences used to fill students with fear. They would nervously wait at home while their parents met with each of their teachers to discuss how well (or not so well) they were doing in school. The information shared between teachers and parents often remained a mystery, until the parents returned home to discuss the conference with their son/daughter.

While conferences still might fill some students with fear, their fear is more likely to be well-earned for this reason: More and more, students are participating in conferences in ways they haven't in past decades. Many schools are not only allowing students to tag along with their parents to conferences, but are also insistent that students have a voice in the conversation. This is a monumental shift in education, one that values participatory education and self-evaluation.

Twenty years ago, assessment and grading could be grouped under two broad headings—report cards and conferences. The report card told parents whether or not their son or daughter had mastered each subject area. Conferences were a sort of verbal report card that defended the written one. There was very

little dialogue. The teacher gave the parents either a favorable or unfavorable report, which was then reported back to the student. True discussion generally occurred only when the conference was called as a last resort because of unresolved difficulties.

Today, students in even the earliest grades are valued participants in conferences. Conferences between teacher, parents, and student at the end of a marking period might have an element of assessment in them, though not if the student holds in her hand a progress report with a grade already on it. These conferences more than likely are a conversation about where a student has been and where she's going. Talking with a student and her parents adds layers onto what you already know about this student as a learner in your classroom. Conferences are an effective means for gathering together the key players in a student's success in order to assess the student's progress and to set goals for the future. In my experience, this only happens when the student is present and active in the conversation.

Conferencing with Your Students

Conversations between a student and her teacher occur informally and formally throughout the year. Formal conversations might be characterized as those which have assessment as the purpose or one of the stated purposes. Figure 12 (page 35) is a sample Teacher/Student Conference Form. A form like this can give the conversation some structure and provide a space to jot down quotes or questions you want to remember. After your conversation, make a copy and give one to your student.

About Their Work

Heath and Mangiola (1991) write that "assessment that is authentic must actively engage students so that they understand not only what they know, but also how they can learn more and do so more effectively" (p. 46). Standardized tests with multiple choice questions do not fit into this definition of authentic assessment. While scores from multiple choice tests might tell students what they know—or what questions they know the answers to—they fail to inform them of how they can learn more and do so more effectively.

Teacher/Student Conference Notes

Student: _____ Date: _____

Purpose of conference

_____

_____

What we talked about

_____

_____

_____

_____

Student's response and follow-up

_____

_____

_____

_____

Teacher's response and follow-up

_____

_____

_____

Date and plan for next formal conversation

_____

_____

Figure 12

About Their Portfolios

When a student and teacher sit down to discuss a portfolio, the stage is set for both to engage in authentic assessment. Often, a student needs to be guided to be self-reflective about his writing. You can do this by asking him direct questions about his writing during the conference. Students need to learn the skill of self-critiquing. Milner and Milner (1993) list "conferencing with student writers as a basic feature of instruction" in the process approach to writing (p. 265). Conferring means "finding out what students are discovering they want to say and helping them reflect on effective ways of saying it" (p. 266). When writing, a student uses one dimension of his voice. Part of what teachers of writing do is work with students to develop a voice that is unique to them. The development of this voice is one characteristic of growth as a writer. When speaking about his writing with his teacher, a writer gets a second opportunity to express his thoughts and intentions. Conferring in this way adds another dimension to a student's work. This conversation should not simply be an explanation of what he *meant* to say;

his writing should do that on its own. Sometimes, by talking about a piece of writing, a student realizes he needs to go back and work with it more so that it doesn't need the support of his explanation. Talking about a piece of writing with a teacher engages the student in self-assessment and allows the teacher to share observations to help make him the best writer he can be. Below are some questions teachers can ask during a conference that help, as Milner and Milner put it, teachers "find out what students are discovering they want to say," and that might help students to "reflect on effective ways of saying it." Figure 13 (page 37) provides questions for use with individual pieces of writing.

- What do you like best about this writing?

- What needs improvement?

- How did you select your portfolio pieces?

- What are you proudest of in this portfolio?

- What does your portfolio say about you as a person, writer, and student?

- How would you grade this portfolio?

Questions That Invite Student Reflection

Name _____ Date _____

Project/written assignment on which you are reflecting: _____

_____

1. How did you plan this piece? _____

2. Tell me about the process of creating it. _____

_____

3. Does your final product accurately reflect your initial idea? Did this turn out like you imagined it would? _____

4. List the three most significant things you've learned in doing this assignment.

_____

5. In what ways are you pleased with it? _____

_____

6. In what ways are you frustrated with it? _____

_____

7. What questions do you have that you want to discuss? _____

_____

8. What have you learned about yourself as a person and/or student in the process of creating this piece? _____

_____

9. What can I or another reader learn about you from looking at this piece?

_____

10. Do you think this piece reflects the best you can do? Why or why not?

_____

11. If you could do this piece again, would you do anything differently? Why or why not? _____

Figure 13

Taping Conversations

You can also conduct authentic assessment through the taping of conversations. Verbal assessment has long been used in foreign language classrooms, as well as in English-as-a-Second-Language instruction. Because a gut-level, general feeling about how a student is progressing in learning a language, though probably quite accurate, is hard to document, teachers are finding other ways to note growth in their students' oral communication. They are doing this by audiotaping their group conversations (Heath and Mangiola, 1991).

Heath and Mangiola describe how students in an ESL classroom transcribe recordings of small-group conversations, then evaluate participants' effectiveness in helping the group problem-solve and achieve its task. Their evaluation is done on a coding chart created by the students (Figure 14, page 39). "Students defined successful conversations as those during which speakers were engaged with and knowledgeable about the topic of the conversation, considerate of other speakers, and capable of both expressing their own thoughts clearly and building from the ideas of others" (p. 42).

Though not directly involving the teacher in assessment, this activity nonetheless invites students to assess their own and each other's oral language communication skills. This activity can be reproduced and extended when the teacher listens to these taped conversations and fills in a coding sheet herself. Additionally, coding sheets from group conversations at different points in the school year can be included in a student's portfolio as documentation of her oral language growth.

Coding Sheet from an Intermediate English-as-a-Second-Language Class

Each time you hear one of the following on the tape, place a check mark under the speaker's name. For #6, give one check for **a**, two checks for **b**, and three for **c**.

Students:	Angelica	Lucia	Marco	Kim
1. Successful interruption or break into talk of someone who speaks too long	____	____	____	____
2. Asking a question (this includes saying, "I don't know. Can you tell me?")	____	____	____	____
3. Correcting an error in English quickly—without many "uh, uhs"	____	____	____	____
4. Building what you say from what someone else in the group has said	____	____	____	____
5. Helping someone else get a turn to talk ("What do you think, Lee?")	____	____	____	____
6. Asking for clarification a. "Huh?" "What?"	____	____	____	____
b. "Would you say that again?"	____	____	____	____
c. "Do you mean (paraphrase of what was said)?"	____	____	____	____
7. Referring to the source of information (telling from where an idea came)	____	____	____	____

Figure 14

Chapter 6

Reading Journals

For many years before *authentic* became the adjective that needed to be attached to assessment in order to give it legitimacy, people have been talking and writing about books. Over a meal, in the living room, on the beach, online, on the subway—readers talk about books. If we want our students to be lifelong readers, then we need to get them reading and talking about books from childhood on.

When I first started teaching, someone recommended a book about reading and writing workshops in the middle school classroom. The ideas and practical applications I found in that now-classic book, *In the Middle* by Nancie Atwell, guided the way I set up my classroom and taught my students. Every summer before teaching, I reread the book and adapted what I read to my own classroom. The ways I conduct reading and writing workshops in the various schools in which I have taught— from the Bronx in New York City to a public college preparatory school in Michigan—shift

depending on the needs of my students and the curriculum. But letting students choose their own books to read, giving them time to read in class, using reading journals, and keeping a Status of the Class reading chart, as laid out by Atwell, are components of my English class that do not change. Much of the information here is borrowed and adapted from her.

In my classroom, these components of a reading workshop are not separated from assessment. They *are* the assessment tools I use.

At the beginning of the school year, I ask my students to fill out **reading and writing surveys**. These surveys give me an idea of how they learned to read, what kinds of books and authors they like, how many books they typically read in a year, and some of their general attitudes toward reading. This is my first picture of my students as readers. That same survey, given at the end of the year, is typically my last. Much transpires between those two surveys, which serve as markers of the growth of my students as readers during the course of the year.

Because most of the schools in which I taught do not have libraries, I have built up a modest classroom library of my own over the years. Students are free to browse through or check out the books. We have silent reading the first twenty minutes of every class.

Those students who bring in a book settle right into reading. Those who don't, browse through the class library. At the beginning of the year, I observe the students in order to "read" their reading behavior—who always brings a book? Who always forgets a book? Who seems disinterested in finding a book? How can I link what students are interested in with particular books? In this way, I get a glimpse of the real-world reading habits of my students. This observation, coupled with the reading surveys, gives me a fuller picture of who my students are as readers. The **Class Reading Record** (Figure 15, page 44) provides a space to formally record my observations.

Documenting What Students Are Reading

Once the students have settled into reading, I circulate around the class with the Class Reading Record, a clipboard, and a pen. As unobtrusively as possible, I look over each student's shoulder to see what book he is reading and what page he is on. I write these down under the day's date and next to the student's name on the Reading Record. If a student is on the same page as the day before, I quietly ask why. If I notice he is reading a new book, I'll ask if he finished reading his last one, or if he abandoned it. When I am finished, I sit at my desk and take a few minutes to look over the record.

I use highlighters to clarify this picture of my students' reading. I highlight in green books that students have completed. I highlight in yellow things that might concern me were they to continue: for example, if Marcos reads the beginnings of three different books in as many days, or if Carl forgets his book at home, or if Tanya is on the same page two days in a row. If the behavior continues, I highlight that day in red, which means I need to talk with that student. Highlighting in this manner allows me to closely monitor and assess *how, what,* and *how often* my students are reading. It also takes the guesswork out of wondering who's keeping up with her reading and who is not, especially when we read one book as a whole class.

Over the course of a semester, the Reading Record documents the reading lives of my students. At the end of the semester when they list all the books they've read, it eliminates any surprises because my students know I've kept track of what they've been reading—or haven't been reading—all semester. I refer to the record during conferences when I ask students to have a conversation about what they've read, and how they've grown as readers.

Class list	10-2-05	10-3-05	10-4-05
Diana	Melville, p. 37	Melville, p. 37	
Marcus	L'Engle, p. 116	L'Engle, p. 123	L'Engle, p. 131
Luke	MacLachlan, p. 6	Lewis, p. 5	Konigsburg, p. 9

In addition to the Class Reading Record, my students fill out **Individual Reading Records** (Atwell, 1993). These document which books they've read, when they either abandoned or finished each one, and the genre of each book (Figure 16, page 45). During our end-of-the-semester conference, I ask the students to analyze their reading lives and look for any patterns that emerged. By adding to their Individual Reading Records every time they finish or abandon a book, students don't have to estimate whether or not they're meeting the class reading requirement determined by you. Figure 17 (page 46) shows a sample **Reading Checklist** I hand out to every student, and which they each hand back to me at the end of the year.

The Class and Individual Reading Records document and reveal what kinds of books students read, what kinds of books they abandon, and how many books they've read. It doesn't assess how well students comprehend what they're reading. For that, I use Reading Journals.

Writing Literary Letters

Reading journals give space for written dialogues about literature. In them, students can question, admire, and connect with literature and language and with other learners. When done well, the contents of a student's reading journal provide invaluable insight into how a student reads, processes what she reads, and responds to what she reads.

Reading journals also alter the usual teacher/student talk. They are not comments a teacher writes in response to a student; they are literary letters. In reading journals, you hear the voices of students who might otherwise not speak up in your classroom. The written dialogue between and with my students in their reading journals has always been one of my favorite things to read.

Class Reading Record

Class List	Date:	Date:	Date:	Date:	Date:

Figure 15 (Adapted from Atwell, 1998).

0-7696-4076-1 *Classroom Assessment*

Individual Reading Record for _____

#	Title	Author	Genre	Date finished	Date abandoned
1					
2					
3					
4					
5					
6					
7					
8					
9					
10					
11					
12					
13					
14					
15					
16					
17					
18					
19					
20					
21					
22					
23					
24					

Figure 16 (Adapted from Atwell, 1998).

0-7696-4076-1 *Classroom Assessment*

Quantity, Range, and Depth of Reading Checklist:

Every middle school English student must read at least 24 books this year. That means you should read at least twelve books by the end of the first semester. Here is a list of the kinds of reading I expect you to do this year. Staple this sheet to the back cover of your reading journal and check off each task as you accomplish it.

___ At least 24 books or their equivalent in articles, newspapers, or textbooks over the course of the year. (Your history textbook will count for one book, and each novel we read together in class may also be counted.) In order to count toward the requirement, books must be appropriate for your individual reading level and of high quality. Ask if you're not sure! List each one on your Reading Record.

___ At least three different genres of printed materials (novels, short stories from a magazine, poetry, etc.).

___ Works by at least five different authors.

Authors' names: _____

_____

_____

_____

_____

___ At least four books (or book equivalents) on one issue or subject, in one genre, or by a single author. List them below.

_____

_____

_____

_____

Author, issue/subject, or genre: _____

You must read at least twelve books and be halfway through this checklist by the end of the first semester in December. I will hold a conference with each of you then. At that time, we'll make a reading plan for second semester based on what you've read so far.

Figure 17

The writing found in a reading journal speaks to the personal, intellectual, and dialogic nature of learning. It enforces the idea that learning is a social process, and that language is a social construct. Specific entries or letters in a reading journal are not edited or graded by the teacher, though the effort a student has put into her reading journal will probably be evaluated at different points throughout the year. Instead, the reading journal creates a place for those students whose voices are rarely part of a conversation. They create a place for students to think and write critically about—and make connections with —the "word and the world" (Shor and Friere, 1987).

In our literary letters, my students and I argue, wonder, recommend, and share stories. There is something about the format of writing letters that creates particularly rich exchanges between readers, in part because the exchanges are personal and authentic. I do not ask my students questions I know the answers to, nor do I test my students as I write by throwing in some comprehension questions. This exchange of ideas does not happen magically, of course.

I spend as much time as needed at the beginning of the year carefully explaining the purposes of reading journals. We also explore the variety of ways to respond to literature. I write them a letter describing the kinds of things I want them to write about in a literary letter. "Write about what you're reading. Tell what you noticed. Tell what you thought, felt, and why. Tell what you liked, and be vocal about what you didn't. Ask questions." And I conduct mini-lessons throughout the year with individuals and the whole class about what goes into a thoughtful literary letter.

Much writing has been done on the use of reading journals in the English classroom. I have borrowed heavily from Atwell's model both in my work with students and here. I highly recommend her book, *In the Middle*, which not only explores theoretical reasons behind reading journals, but also clearly lays out how to implement both reading journals and reading and writing workshops in your classroom.

What I Learn from Literary Letters

As a bare minimum for passing, I require students to write at least two literary letters a week in their own journals. Responding to letters in other students' journals doesn't count toward this requirement. And though I hope students will write to me more often, I ask them to write a literary letter to me at least every other week.

In my grade book each year, I create four columns where I record how many letters each student has written. There are two columns for the midterms and two for the ends of the semesters. However, quantity of letters is not what I'm looking for. In fact, I become concerned when I see a student writing letters every day during silent reading time. More often than not, writing letters is an avoidance technique for this student, and the letters she writes have little literary worth. The goal is for students to engage in written dialogues with each other and, to some extent, the texts, in order to make sense of the text, their world, and themselves as readers.

A student of mine once wondered about the way an author began a particular story. This wondering revealed the depth of his interaction with the text:

"What was the author thinking when he began <u>What Jamie Saw</u> *with that baby being flung across the room and that kid Jamie seeing the whole thing? I've never read a book that started that way, and I never want to again, because its too real and you're not sure if it really happened or not. You just can't put it down…."* I could tell a lot about this student as a reader from what he wrote.

▌ He feels confident enough to question the way the author so graphically wrote his lead: *What was the author thinking?*

▌ He probably finished the book in a short period of time: *You just can't put it down.*

▌ One of this student's criteria for compelling writing is that it is realistic: *It's too real and you're not sure if it really happened or not.*

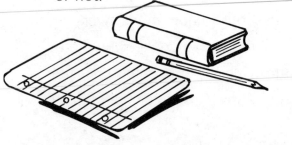

- Realistic fiction can be disturbing, perhaps too disturbing, for this student: *I've never read a book that started that way, and I never want to again.*

- Despite the jarring lead, this student continued to read: *You just can't put it down.*

- *What Jamie Saw* is unlike most of the fiction this student has read: *I've never read a book that started that way*.

- Finally, because I just can't help myself, I notice that this student leaves out the apostrophe in *its*. The reading journal is **not** the place to correct or even point out grammatical errors, but I do write *its/it's* in my notebook. This is where I keep a running list of possible reading and writing mini-lessons to teach.

Note: In reading the excerpt from this literary letter, I have a wondering of my own: This student reacted quite strongly to the (fictional) abuse described in the beginning of *What Jamie Saw*. I wonder if this is indicative of compelling writing, or if his reaction is informed by personal experience with abuse? I'll keep this in the back of my mind for the rest of the year, observing this student and continuing to assess him.

Why did I include a wondering like this in a book on assessment? If I'm really trying to look holistically at each student—at who they are, their prior knowledge and experiences, what they know, how they learn, how they show what they know—then it would be careless of me to ignore the vague, but nagging, worry that my student brings personal experience to this particular reading.

It's easier to notice the grammatical mistakes, such as the missing apostrophe. Teachers don't do the kind of messy assessment described above. We are not social workers. But this doesn't mean that we should ignore a warning sign. If you find yourself wondering about a particular student the way I did, share your concerns with someone in your school who is qualified to assess students in ways you are not and should not.

Reading Journals in Other Classes

Reading journals are not the exclusive property of English classrooms. They can be used in history, foreign language, ESL, and even science classes. It's just that they work particularly well in classes in which students are reading a variety of texts simultaneously. What makes them different from learning log journals is the open-ended quality of dialogue found in the letters. In reading journals, students do not respond in writing to a particular question posed by the teacher. Every letter is unique, and, on any given day, you will have about thirty different letters and about as many different books being read and responded to by your students. Capitalize on the popularity of instant messaging and have your students write letters to others outside your class via email. Ask that they print them out once a week and stick them in a binder or folder so they have a hard copy of their correspondence.

Evaluating Reading Journals

Assessing these letters will require a dynamic rubric that can be created collaboratively with students well before the end of each marking period. In other words, the beginning-of-the-year letters probably will—and should—differ in quality from those written near the end of the year. With your students, you should create a list, as Atwell does, of all the topics students are writing about in their literary letters throughout the year. The list that results from this meta-cognitive thinking will grow as the year progresses and can be used in creating the rubric by which the reading journals are assessed.

Chapter 7

Learning Logs

"Learning logs differ from journals in their focus on the students' reflections on their own learning" (Milner and Milner, 1993).

Learning logs are another way to get your students engaged in self-assessment. Learning logs are not simply places to record what students are doing or observing. Instead, learning logs invite students to become researchers of their own work by inviting them to *learn* from what they're doing or observing in their reading, writing, and discussions.

Learning logs, reader response journals, and reading journals are all different writing-to-learn strategies. Students use writing to learn and to make sense of what they're learning. Learning logs differ from reading journals in that the writing students do in them generally focuses on a shared text. Many of the entries in a learning log will be responses to a direct question or wondering posed by you and your students.

In contrast to talking about a text, writing slows down the thinking process, making it more deliberate. In the pages of learning logs, "students are able to explore their ideas and feelings, to contemplate how the text evoked certain responses, and to formulate hypotheses, predictions, and questions about their reading, without worrying about errors" (Wolman-Bonilla, 1991). As with literary letters, assessment is based on the quality of thought and the content of the learning log responses, not grammatical perfection. There are definitely places where editing counts—final draft pieces in a portfolio, term papers, or other pieces of published writing—but I don't think writing-to-learn responses is one of them.

Writing to Learn

In learning logs, students respond to prompts that are either teacher or student generated. These prompts can be open-ended or quite specific. Here are some examples that show the variety of learning log prompts:

- Think on paper about what concerns and problems you see in your community.

- Does seeing one's own group as "good" necessarily mean that other groups are "bad"?

- Respond to this quote: "Violence just puts more problems in your hand."

- What are the two most important concepts or ideas you've learned about in this unit?

- Write a response to the transcript of the class discussion we had yesterday.

- When you don't understand something you read in your textbook, what do you do?

- If given the chance, how would you teach this concept differently?

- Jot down three quotes from your reading that stick with you, and explain why you want to remember them.

These prompts invite students to reflect, engage in meta-cognitive thinking, and evaluate. But they also do more than that—they invite students into the collective conversation and affirm that learning is a social action. In reading your students' learning logs, you'll discover that the student who never volunteers to speak in class shows a surprising amount of insight when she writes to learn. The student who seems to take very little seriously might respond quite seriously to the prompt you've given. This doesn't mean that your students' learning log responses will always surprise you, but for some students—usually the quiet ones—writing in learning logs gives you and them the opportunity to draw from the silent but deep wells of thought in them.

Sometimes in my classes, small groups will each choose a novel to read. Usually the novels have similar themes, but sometimes I'll simply choose five novels and students sign up to read the one that most interests them. For the next few weeks, they meet regularly with the other members of their small group who are reading the same book. They create a calendar of their reading schedule, assign a task to each person, such as log recorder or discussion facilitator, and have book talks. I've found that a group learning log works well in this kind of setting where every student has ownership of the group. When students meet, each is required to bring their book, reading journal, and calendar. The group's learning log is the responsibility of the person who is assigned to write that day's entry.

At times I give each group a prompt (or perhaps all groups the same prompt) to which they respond in their learning log. Some days the learning log entries are based on what students have written on sticky notes while reading the night before. A learning log might be an extension of one person's idea, or an attempt to answer a question they have as a group. I try not to let learning logs morph into logs that simply record the events of the book talk. I collect and read these learning logs weekly. They let me listen in on each group's conversation in a closer way than I can when there are five groups having five different conversations simultaneously.

Of course, I do listen in on book talks. I spend my time meandering around the class listening and observing and answering questions when asked. I try not to interrupt, though I do enjoy sitting down and entering into the conversation. The danger with sitting down is that it's natural for my students to look to me as the discussion facilitator. It's important to not slip into this role.

When students in a book talk group know they will all receive the same grade for each learning log entry, they tend to contribute more than they would if only the person writing the learning log were to receive the grade. Working collaboratively to write a learning log takes negotiation, participation, and patience on the part of students. In that way, it very much reflects life outside the classroom.

Learning Logs Across the Curriculum

Learning logs are one of the more adaptable tools of assessment around. In his biology class, R. Tierney (1990) uses the following system of learning logs to increase his students' understanding of the topic on which he's just lectured. On one side of a notebook page, students take notes as he lectures. When he's finished, students "write" what amounts to a learning log in three parts: First, they briefly recap the notes in their own words; second, they answer the question "so what?" below the recap; third, they sketch a diagram of a figural representation of what has just been taught (Milner and Milner, p. 311).

Here are some other ideas:

- Write a response to a prompt while reading a novel in a foreign language class.

- Write a response to a postcard prompt in art.

- Write a prediction for how a science experiment will turn out.

- Respond to a political ad.

- Write a response to a small group discussion about the differences between a democracy and a dictatorship, or between socialism and capitalism.

- Write a story problem in math.

- Write a mathematical proof as a haiku.

Evaluating Learning Log Entries

Assessing the writing done in learning logs has always been for me a two-part process. I find it too time-consuming to thoughtfully respond to each learning log my students write, but I do collect each one and read it. In my class, learning logs are written on loose-leaf sheets of paper for this very purpose, and so that they aren't confused with Reading Journals.

Other teachers I've known like to use composition notebooks because they more closely resemble a real log. Use what works for you. The rubric for assessing the learning logs changes with each entry. Obviously, the criteria for a thoughtful response to a vignette in *The House on Mango Street* are completely different from a response to the prompt, "What surprised you in the course of conducting your I-Search?"

After reading, I give each entry an evaluation number from 1–3, with 1 showing the least amount of effort and 3 showing the most. Clearly, this is not an exact science. About once a month, I take the time to respond in writing to learning logs. Sometimes I'll collect them as usual and respond to them over the weekend. Or I'll ask students to hand in a learning log entry they really want me to respond to. Other times I'll invite them to choose their best learning log. At different points during the year I'll hand out a learning log I've written and ask them to evaluate it with a 1–3 mark and respond to it.

This almost always results in a rich discussion about what a thoughtful learning log looks like, how much time it takes to respond intelligently to someone's writing, how difficult it is to grade, and how important it is to know what you're looking for when you evaluate a piece of writing.

Entering into this *dialogic curriculum*[1] is important for me. I don't always want to be the teacher. I want and expect my students to teach each other, me, and themselves. I want them to actively engage with and question what they're learning,

talk back to it, and evaluate it. Learning logs provide the blank pages for them to do so.

Writing a Response to Literature

When my students and I read a novel together, I take the opportunity to teach them another way to respond to literature besides learning logs and literary letters. Because we are all quite literally on the same page, it makes sense for me to introduce literary analysis to middle school students.

When I teach students how to specifically write a response to literature, I've found it helpful to give them the following guidelines:

1st paragraph: Briefly retell the events of a particular section of the text. This contextualizes the rest of your response. "In this section of the novel…" (Most book reports only retell the plot. Students who are used to writing book reports as a response to literature find it challenging to condense and confine their retelling to one paragraph.)

[1] Thanks to Patricia Stock's *The Dialogic Curriculum: Teaching and Learning in a Multicultural Society* for this phrase.

2nd paragraph: Write your wonderings, predictions, and questions about the plot, author's style of writing, character's thoughts, and actions.

3rd paragraph: Make a judgment. State and explain your opinion of the plot, characters, or specific events in the story. Tell what you think about the author's writing style.

4th paragraph: Explain how a theme of the text is presented and illustrated in this section of the book. Use a quote to support this.

5th paragraph: Make connections between the text and another text, the text and yourself, and the text and the world (historical and/or current events).

This is a progressive learning activity that I usually introduce through a series of mini-lessons when we read our first novel together. Figure 18 shows how I asked students to practice writing a response to literature when we read William Golding's *Lord of the Flies* as a class.

For chapters 1 and 2—write a one-paragraph summary of each chapter. Make every word count.

For chapters 3 and 4—add a paragraph about your wonderings to the summary paragraphs. These can be wonderings about what is going on in the book, why characters act a specific way, or why the author writes as he does (two paragraphs for each chapter).

For chapter 5—add a paragraph to the other two (summary and wonderings) that includes connections you are making. These can be text-text, text-self, and text-world connections (three paragraphs for chapter 5).

Figure 18

As we add layers to our responses to literature, they become richer and go deeper because they require students to dig into the text, to compare and contrast texts, and to ask questions. If a goal for my students is to get them independently using assessment tools, then I've found that teaching them how to write a response to literature provides a tool that effectively helps them analyze and make sense of what they read. Students must be actively engaged with the text in order to write a decent response to literature. This is in contrast to the minimal energy required to write a book report, which is not only boring to read because the student doesn't bring any new information to the response, but is also, at best, uninspiring, and at worst, copied from the Internet.

Evaluating a Response to Literature

By the end of the first semester, when I ask my students to write a response to literature, they know what it requires. They know I expect a solid page of thought, and in their notes they have the rubric for what goes into a thoughtful response. I usually assign each paragraph of a response a grade of 1–3, with 3 being the highest. This gives each full response to literature fifteen points, which carries enough weight to show I value their thoughts and the work they put into their writing.

Chapter 8

Finding Time for Assessment

I've never heard a teacher say that he has too much time on his hands. Most every teacher feels pressed for time on a daily basis. A lot of this pressure comes from the nearly endless task of assessment. Rarely will you hear a teacher complain about having to produce yet another lesson to teach. More than likely, complaints revolve around the piles of papers, mountains of grading, and hours of responding that are all part of the process of education and assessment. Without assessment, we'd have no measure of the effectiveness of what we're teaching, nor would we know what or how well our students were learning. Assessment is one way students communicate with us. Without it, teachers might as well teach to a video camera.

The question is not whether to engage in assessment, but *how* and *which kinds* of assessment to use. Each teacher needs to find the kinds that work best for her students at a given time and on a given subject, while adhering to state and national standards. It's a daunting task. It takes years to find what works and to create a balance.

I cannot prescribe a time-management method that will work for you. You'll have to do that on your own. I can only tell you what's worked for me and for other teachers, and hope that you find some nuggets of helpful information to adapt to your own classroom, school environment, and teaching style. In the beginning …

1. Make a map.
2. Decide how you'll assess.
3. Start making copies of …
   - *Reading and Writing Survey*
   - *Class Reading Record (p. 44)*
   - *Individual Reading Record (p. 45)*
   - *Quantity, Range, and Depth of Reading Checklist (p. 46)*
   - *Goals for Fluent Readers (p. 31)*
   - Letter introducing *Reading Journals and Literary Letters (p. 32)*
   - Writing Folders
   - *Individual Writing Record (p. 14)*
   - Editing Checklists
   - *Observation Checklist (p. 26)*
4. Write …
   - Beginning-of-the-Year Letter
   - Syllabus
5. Get to know the grading system.

1. Make a map.

Before the school year starts, I make a map of the year. I look at what my state and national standards tell me that my kids need to know by the end of the year. I write the name of each month on a page and brainstorm some ideas about what units or projects we'll study. Since I teach English, I list which books we'll read, and which genres of writing I want my students to try. Then I dedicate a page for each month of the year we're in school, and get more specific about what we'll do each month. On these pages I assign a place for everything. For example, I've learned by trial and error that I-Searches do not take two weeks, as I thought they would before I tried them during my second year of teaching. They take a good month, and I think they work best after spring break and before preparation for final examinations begins.

Under each major unit, project, shared reading, or writing, I write down the kind of assessment(s) I think will work best for what I want my students to learn. This is somewhat fluid, and somewhat based on common sense. Giving a multiple choice test does not seem to me to be a wise way to assess how well students comprehend what they have read. In some schools at which I taught, our students' performances on state tests determined whether or not the school would remain open or be shut down by the state. Whatever you believe about the validity of standardized tests in assessing learning becomes moot under this kind of pressure. When the stakes are that high, it isn't an option to not have the time to prepare your students for testing. So I build time for that into my map of the year, as well.

2. *Decide how you'll assess.*

As much as possible, I try to use authentic assessment in my classroom. This means that the ways in which I assess student comprehension and work are close to the ways in which they do—and will in the future—make sense of what they learn in the real world. I want to make space for my students to have conversations about literature the way adults do in book groups. Instead of researching a question somebody else has already answered, I invite my students to conduct I-Searches about real-life questions they have.

One student I had in New York wrote an I-Search on how breast cancer metastasizes. He was interested in learning more about it because his aunt had just been diagnosed with breast cancer. A group of eighth-grade girls in the Bronx wanted to know why teenage pregnancy was such a problem in their community, so they spent the school year conducting interviews, forming a study group, and doing research on teen pregnancy. At the end of the year, they published an informational booklet that was distributed to their peers. Had I chosen a topic for them, the intensity and urgency with which they studied this topic would have been absent, and I don't think their study would have sustained itself for an entire school year and beyond.

Examples like these seem to me to be authentic assessment at its best. It's important for me to make space for them in my classroom. Publishing a piece of writing—and all the work a student does in the process—means very little if the only person who reads the published piece is a teacher with a big red pen poised to correct spelling mistakes. Knowing that they'll share their published pieces with a larger audience of peers and parents ups the ante and gives purpose to the hard work they do drafting, revising, editing, and typing.

3. Start copying.

I mull over how to mark what we learn with authentic assessment as I map out the year. When I have a map that takes me where I want to go with my students, I do the busy work of getting everything set before school starts. Here is a partial list of what I want to have on hand before the beginning of the school year:

▪ A **Reading and Writing Survey** for each student to complete at the beginning of the year. I make two copies of each of these and save one to administer at the end of the year.

▪ A stack of **Class Reading Record** sheets clipped onto a separate clipboard for each section I teach. I wait to write student names on them until the second day of school—I know students will drop and add my course.

▪ Two copies of the **Individual Reading Record** for each student. They will staple these to the inside covers of their Reading Journals.

▪ A **Quantity, Range, and Depth of Reading Checklist** for each student.

▪ A **Goals for Fluent Readers** handout for each student. On it, students record personal reading fluency goals for the year. At our year-end individual conferences, students and I refer to this in assessing growth over the year.

▪ A copy of **a letter introducing Reading Journals and Literary Letters** that I will hand out to students sometime in the first week.

▪ **Writing Folders** in a different color for each section. These stay in the class, filed in a box. In these folders are kept the pieces of writing my students have either finished or published, which are too important to risk losing.

▪ Two copies of **Individual Writing Records** for each student. These get stapled to the inside of their writing folders.

▪ An **Editing Checklist** for each folder.

▪ A stack of **Observation Checklists** clipped to a clipboard. I hole-punch these so that after I do observations I can immediately file them in my own three-ring binder, which is divided by class.

■ A **three-ring binder for each section** I teach, clearly labeled with the name or number of the section. All the handouts I give are dated and go into these binders so that students who are absent have access to everything we've done in class and can take or make copies for their own binders. At the end of the year, the binder serves as a sort of learning log of the past year, and I refer to it in creating a map of the next year. I've always wanted to have somebody record what we did in every class and include that in the binder as well, but I've never managed to do that consistently.

4. Write . . .

■ A **Beginning-of-the-Year Letter** to my students, in which I introduce myself and try to reveal some detail about myself that I think my students don't already know. Writing a letter back to me about themselves is my students' first assignment of the year. I want to start a written conversation right off the bat. Reading their letters not only tells me more about who they are, but also gives me an idea of how comfortable my students are with writing.

■ A **syllabus** that is a draft of what we'll learn during the course of the year. Though I usually choose a few novels I know we'll read together, and a few projects everyone will do, there's some room for us to create the map together as we go. In addition to letting students know what we'll basically be doing in class, the syllabus also gives them requirements and a rough break-down of my grading system. For instance, students must read at least 24 books throughout the year in order to meet the reading requirement. I want them to know that up front so they can get started immediately. The syllabus explains how they can earn extra points for each book they read beyond the original 24.

5. Get to know the grading system.

■ Finally, I set up **a grading system** that works for me. When I began teaching, it was a grade book that went everywhere with me. Now I use an electronic grading system, but I still carry a grade book with me when I take work home. Whatever it is that you use, I suggest you familiarize yourself with it before the school year begins.

These are some of the assessment tools I prepare well in advance of the first day of school. I do this early because I know I won't have the time once school begins. You will obviously have different tools you'll use. In any case, assessment will not seem so overwhelming if you have several tools on hand before you need them.

The more organized I am, the easier it is for me to find time for assessment during the school year. In addition to getting ready before the school year begins, I find that two activities in particular make assessment less overwhelming during the school year. First, I take some time before the start of each school day to file observations from the previous day in my personal binder. I also put a copy of any handouts I intend to give in each class's binder. After doing that, I input any grades I have into the computer. Secondly, after school I make sure I have enough Observation Checklists and Reading Records for the next day. I make copies of these and any handouts so I don't have to elbow my way through the crowd by the copier in the morning. I also input any grades given during the day. These are generally quick grades given for completed homework, spelling quizzes, or daily class work. These grades do not require extensive responses or time to compute.

This before and after school work makes assessment more manageable for me. It also frees up my planning period to read and respond to literary letters or plan for the next day. Of course, there are going to be times during the year—midterms, final examinations, progress reports—when assessment cannot neatly fit into your schedule. Instead, your schedule must fit into your assessment. I expect to work one or two very late nights during midterms and at the end of each semester in order to complete my grading and write narrative report cards. I've found that including these late nights into the expectations I have of the school year makes the lost sleep seem much less painful.

Bibliography

Anthony, R.J., Johnson, T.D., Mickelson, N.I., & Preece, A. (1991). *Evaluating Literacy: A Perspective for Change*. Portsmouth, NH: Heinemann.

Atwell, N. (1998) *In the Middle: New Understandings About Writing, Reading, and Learning*, 2nd edition. Portsmouth, NH: Boynton/Cook.

Claggett, F. (1996). *A Measure of Success*. Portsmouth, NH: Boynton/Cook.

Elbow, P. (1986). *Embracing Contraries: Explorations in Learning and Teaching*. New York: Oxford University Press.

Gere, A.R., Fairbanks, C., Howes, A., Roop, L., & Schaafsma, D. (1992). *Language and Reflection: An Integrated Approach to Teaching English*. New York: Macmillan.

Graham, J. (1997)."The Way Things Work," from *The Dream of the Unified Field*. New York: Ecco.

Graves, D. (1991). *The Reading/Writing Teacher's Companion: Build a Literate Classroom*. Portsmouth, NH: Heinemann-Boynton/Cook.

Heath, S. B., & Mangiola, L. (1991). *Children of Promise: Literate Activity in Linguistically and Culturally Diverse Classrooms* (1991). Washington, D.C.: National Education Association.

McDonald, J., Mohr, N., Dichter, A., & McDonald, E. (2003). *The Power of Protocols: An Educator's Guide to Better Practice*. New York: Teachers College Press.

Milner, J.O., & Milner, L.M. (1993). *Bridging English*. New York: Macmillan.

Moffet, J., & Wagner, B.J. (1976). *Student-Centered Language Arts and Reading, K-13: A Handbook for Teachers* (2nd edition). Boston: Houghton Mifflin.

Seidel, S. (1998). *Wondering to Be Done: The Collaborative Assessment Conference*. In D. Allen (Ed.), *Assessing Student Learning: From Grading to Understanding* (pp. 21–39). New York: Teachers College Press.

Shor, I., & Friere, P. (1987). *A Pedagogy for Liberation: Dialogues on Transforming Education*. South Hadley, MA: Bergin and Garvey.

Smith. M., & Juska, J. (2001). *The Whole Story: Teachers Talk About Portfolios*. Berkley, CA: National Writing Project.

Tendero, A. (1994). *A View From the Desk: Portfolios, Organization and Control*. Conference paper, Northern Virginia Writing Project.

Tierney, R. (1990, July). *Writing to Learn in Science*. Lecture at Wake Forest University, Winston-Salem, NC.

Wollman-Bonilla, J. (1991). *Response Journals: Inviting Students to Think and Write About Literature*. New York: Scholastic.